GEORGE ORWELL

HAYDN MIDDLETON

Heinemann

www.heinemann.co.uk/library
Visit our website to find out more information about **Heinemann Library** books.

To order:
☎ Phone 44 (0) 1865 888066
▤ Send a fax to 44 (0) 1865 314091
▥ Visit the Heinemann Bookshop at www.heinemann.co.uk/library to browse our
catalogue and order online.

First published in Great Britain by Heinemann Library, Halley Court, Jordan Hill, Oxford
OX2 8EJ, a division of Reed Educational and Professional Publishing Ltd. Heinemann is a
registered trademark of Reed Educational and Professional Publishing Ltd.

OXFORD MELBOURNE AUCKLAND JOHANNESBURG BLANTYRE
GABORONE IBADAN PORTSMOUTH NH (USA) CHICAGO

Designed by Tinstar Design (www.tinstar.co.uk)
Originated by Ambassador Litho Ltd.
Printed and bound by South China Printing Company Ltd in Hong Kong/China

ISBN 0 431 13994 6   (hardback)   ISBN 0 431 14001 4   (paperback)
06 05 04 03 02   07 06 05 04 03
10 9 8 7 6 5 4 3 2 1   10 9 8 7 6 5 4 3 2 1

British Library Cataloguing in Publication Data
Middleton, Haydn
        George Orwell. – (Creative Lives)
        1. Orwell, George, 1903–1950
        2. Novelists, English – 20th century – Biography – Juvenile literature
        I.Title
        823.9'12

Acknowledgements
This book is for Roger Titford.

The Publishers would like to thank the following for permission to reproduce photographs:
BBC: p42; Bridgeman Art Library/Museo Nacional Centro de Arte Reina Sofia, Madrid,
© Succession Picasso/DACS 2002: p34; George Orwell Archive, University College London:
pp5, 6, 8, 13, 23, 26, 33, 37, 38, 41, 43, 52, H. Dakin, pp9, 18, F. de France, p22, Guinever
Buddicom, p11, King-Farlow, p12, Library, pp4, 54, Peter Hort, p47, Roger Beadon, p14,
S. Clair, p51, Vernon Richards, p55; Hulton Archive: pp20, 28, 30; Roger Scruton: p53; Ronald
Grant Archive: pp25, 45, 49; Trevor Clifford Photography: pp17, 21, 35; Waterstone's: p50.

Cover photograph reproduced with permission of AKG London.

Extracts from *Why I Write* (1947), *The Road to Wigan Pier* (1937) and *Coming Up For Air*
(1939) reproduced by permission of Bill Hamilton as the Literary Executor of the Estate of
the late Sonia Brownell Orwell and Secker & Warburg Ltd.

Our thanks to Gillian Furlong for her assistance in the preparation of this book.

Contents

Any words appearing in the text in bold, **like this**, are explained in the Glossary.

'The whole truth'

'George Orwell' was the **pseudonym** of Eric Arthur Blair. Eric was born in 1903 in Bengal, India, which was then a part of the **British Empire**. In 1950, at the age of just 46, he died of **tuberculosis** in a London hospital. By this time, he had become known to millions as an author, journalist and essay writer. His **obituary** in the journal *Tribune* said he was in some ways a quirky, old-fashioned, even Victorian type of Englishman, with high ideals and a strong sense of duty. 'He will be remembered as a writer particularly by *Animal Farm*,' it went on, 'but he should be remembered equally as a man whose **unorthodoxy** was valuable in an age of power worship, who brought to the literature of our age the rare assets of a courageous spirit and a generous mind.'

It is almost impossible to think of Orwell and his work without thinking too of the times he lived in. The first half of the 20th century was, in Orwell's own words, 'a tumultuous, revolutionary age'. He lived through World War I and the **Russian Revolution**, the **Great Depression**, the rule of the **Fascist dictators**, World War II and the start of the **Cold War**. Some writers – especially novelists – try to ignore the outside world and pursue more personal artistic aims in their work. Orwell, who wrote six novels, was not one of these. He often wrote beautifully, and sometimes with great humour, but his very best work was deeply political in its content and aims.

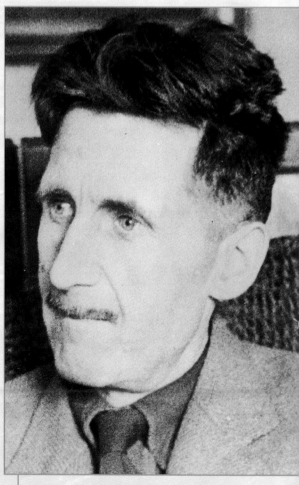

George Orwell in 1945.

George Orwell's baptism certificate, from 1903.

'In a peaceful age,' Orwell wrote, 'I might have written ornate or merely descriptive books, and might have remained almost unaware of my political loyalties. As it is… every line of serious work that I have written since 1936 has been written, directly or indirectly, *against* **totalitarianism** and *for* democratic **Socialism**, as I understand it.' For him, it became impossible to avoid writing about such subjects. After years of struggling to find his true voice as a writer, this political purpose finally sparked his creative genius, and enabled him to produce classic works like *Homage to Catalonia*, *Animal Farm* and *Nineteen Eighty-Four*. But even though they were responses to the political events of his time, his literary skills ensured that they would continue to be read and enjoyed long after the events themselves became a part of history.

The writer's duty

In a 1940 essay, 'Inside the Whale', Orwell wondered what it must have been like for Jonah, the biblical man swallowed alive by a whale: 'The historical Jonah, if he can be so called, was glad enough to escape, but in imagination, in day-dream, countless people have envied him. The whale's belly is simply a womb big enough for an adult. There you are, in the dark, cushioned space that exactly fits you, with yards of blubber between yourself and reality, able to keep up an attitude of the completest indifference, no matter what happens. A storm that would sink all the battleships in the world would hardly reach you as an echo… Short of being dead, it is the final, unsurpassable stage of irresponsibility.' Orwell saw it as the writer's duty not to hide like Jonah inside his whale, frittering away his life as 'a passive accepter of evil'.

5

'Every book is a failure'

Despite a lifetime of poor health, Orwell did a lot besides writing. In his books he was able to draw heavily on his active experiences – as a military policeman in Burma, as a soldier in the Spanish Civil War or as a broadcaster for the BBC. But some people remembered him as an innocent man, almost childlike in his lifelong passion for nature. 'He was an interesting man to go for a country walk with,' his friend Mabel Fierz recalled in 1970, 'because he knew the flowers and the trees, he knew the names of all these things'. He also had a curious and lasting interest in making small explosives. 'I am not able, and do not want,' he once wrote, 'completely to abandon the world-view that I acquired in childhood.'

Orwell was an extremely practical man, who took great pleasure in manual work and gardening. Once, when asked what he liked, he said solid objects and useless information. His intense interest in both enabled him to write very vividly about what he called 'the surface of life'.

" 'His descriptions of objects and scenery have a wonderful exactness and power, he can draw and hold our interest whether he is describing the technique and practice of dish-washing in Paris or a tiger-hunt in Burma… [But] he catches only the outward aspect of human beings, though he does that marvellously well. His directness of approach has its limitations in an over-simple treatment of human character.'
Orwell's friend, the writer Julian Symons (1950) "

He certainly had few illusions about his own status as a writer. He referred to some of his early, less obviously political novels as 'trash' and 'bilge', and later he wrote that 'every book [of mine] is a failure'. Countless readers have since disagreed with him. Some people even believe that he is among the greatest Englishmen who ever lived. But he has been criticized too – and not only by those who do not agree with his **left-wing** views.

Some critics argue that he was so obsessed with politics that he neglected to make his fictional plots and characters really believable, or even interesting. It is true that his non-fiction writing contains some of his clearest, sharpest and most beautiful passages of prose. But whether he was writing novels or book reviews or essays, his aim was always the same: 'to tell the whole truth without violating my literary interests.' Few writers, if any, have matched Orwell's great **integrity**, either in their life or in their work.

Why he wrote

In an essay from 1946 entitled 'Why I Write', Orwell listed four main motives that all prose writers have, in varying degrees, for writing. First there is sheer **egoism**, or 'the desire to seem clever'. Second comes **aesthetic** enthusiasm or 'perception of beauty in the external world… or in words'. Third is historical impulse, by which he meant a desire to 'find out true facts and store them up for the use of posterity'. Last but by no means least comes political purpose, or the 'desire to push the world in a certain direction, to alter other people's idea of the kind of society that they should strive after'.

'Such, Such Were the Joys'

'It has been said that Eric had an unhappy childhood. I don't think this was in the least true, although he did give out that impression himself when he was grown up.' The person who made this remark, in a BBC radio programme in 1960, knew what she was talking about. She was Avril Blair, Eric's sister, who was born five years after him in 1908. Writing later as George Orwell, Eric did make some of his boyhood sound grim. But memories of the fun he had and of the lasting interests he formed were also a source of **nostalgia** to him.

Eric Arthur Blair at the age of six weeks, in the arms of an Indian servant, before his mother brought him from India to England.

There were three Blair children in all; Marjorie, born in 1898, was the eldest. Their parents, Richard Blair and Ida Limouzin, had married in 1896. Ida, eighteen years younger than her husband, had a French mother who came from a family of teak merchants in Burma. Richard was an official in the British **administration** of India. His work in Bengal sounds strange to us today. At that time the drug opium was legally available in India, and huge amounts of money were made shipping it from India to China. The trade produced a profit of £6.5 million – about one-sixth of the British government's total **revenue** for India. Richard Blair's job, in the Opium Department, was to supervise the drug's production for this trade until its abolition in 1913.

Eric with his parents and sister Avril in 1916. His uniformed father was on leave from fighting in World War I.

Far away from father

Eric, born on 25 June 1903, grew up knowing little of his father. While he was still a baby, his mother brought him and Marjorie to England, where they made their home first at Henley-on-Thames in Oxfordshire, then at nearby Shiplake, before moving back to Henley. Eric's parents had not split up; his mother simply preferred to bring up her children in England. Eric's father visited whenever he had leave, and after he retired in 1912 he came home intending to settle finally with the family. But his service in the British army during World War I (1914–18) took him away again, before all the Blairs were able to set up a new home together at Southwold on the Suffolk coast.

In later life Eric quite liked his father, although as a boy he saw him 'simply as a gruff-voiced elderly man forever saying "Don't"'. His mother was a livelier person who was friendly with **suffragettes** and dressed in an artistic way. She named one of their homes 'Ermadale' – using the first two letters of *Eric* and *Marjorie*. The family belonged to what Eric described as 'the lower-upper middle class' – which he said meant 'upper-middle class without money'. But the Blairs had far more money than most English families.

Although he suffered from an early age with bronchitis, Eric led a healthy outdoor life. He loved swimming, climbing trees, **bird-nesting**, fishing and picking blackberries. This love of nature would stay with him throughout his life. His mother also encouraged him to read books. *Gulliver's Travels* by Jonathan Swift was an early favourite, which he never stopped admiring. And by the age of four or five he was writing his own poems; one was about a tiger with 'chair-like teeth' – a phrase that delighted his mother.

Serving time at St Cyprian's

Like many boys of his social class, Eric was sent at the age of eight to a fee-paying boarding school. The school, on the Sussex coast 96 kilometres (60 miles) south of London, was called St Cyprian's, and it was run by a husband-and-wife team called Wilkes.

Henry Longhurst, later a sports journalist, was also a pupil at St Cyprian's. He described it as 'a vast, gabled, red-brick house with a sunken playing-field, complete with cricket pavilion, known as the Armoury, and twenty-five-yard rifle-range'. He also remembered having to eat cold porridge with thick slimy lumps. Once he was actually sick into his bowl, then made to stand at a side table and eat it up. Eric was there until 1917, when he did well enough at his exams to win a **scholarship** to the prestigious public school, Eton College.

He later gave little credit for this success to St Cyprian's. It was there, he believed, that he started learning to reject 'every form of man's **dominion** over man'.

In 'Such, Such Were the Joys' (an essay that was not published in England until 1968, since Eric himself judged it 'too **libellous** to print') he bitterly attacked the Wilkeses and their educational methods. Mrs Wilkes, for example, grabbed Eric's hair so often that he deliberately kept it greasy so she could not pull it so hard. And Mr Wilkes beat him for wetting the bed. But it is hard to know how different St Cyprian's was from many other such schools at that time. We also cannot be sure how mischievous a boy Eric was.

Eric (left) poses beside childhood friends Jacintha and Prosper Buddicom in 1917. He always liked guns, and also made his own gunpowder at home.

Cyril Connolly, another future writer, was a schoolfriend of Eric's. He remembered Eric as 'tall, pale, with his flaccid [slack] cheeks, and a matter-of-fact, **supercilious** voice. He was one of those boys who seem born old.' But he remarked too that 'his eyes were made to glitter with amusement, his mouth for teasing'. Once Eric read an advertisement for a 'cure' for obesity. He replied to the London address, pretending to be female. A woman then sent him several eager letters, advising him to come and consult her. Eric kept writing back until in the end he told her that his own 'obesity' had been cured 'by a rival firm'.

On to Eton

Unhappy or not, Eric did well at his studies at St Cyprian's – despite being 'crammed' with learning 'as cynically as a goose is crammed for Christmas', as he later remarked. He was particularly inspired by his geography and drawing teacher, Robert Sillar, who took the boys on butterfly-hunting trips. And in 1914, soon after the outbreak of World War I, the eleven-year-old Eric wrote a rousing poem that was printed in *The Henley and South Oxfordshire Standard*. The last verse went:

> 'Awake! Oh you young men of England,
> For if, when your country's in need
> You do not enlist by the thousand,
> You truly are cowards indeed.'

The hated Mrs Wilkes was so proud, she made him read it aloud at assembly, in front of all his class-mates.

Eric (far right) fooling about with friends at Eton in 1919.

Eric continued to write poems and stories at Eton where, as a **King's Scholar**, he was expected to excel and probably progress to Oxford or Cambridge University. However, it did not turn out that way. Perhaps Eric needed teachers like the Wilkeses to keep him

Eric is at the top left in this Eton team picture from 1921. The boys were about to take part in a traditional sport with bewildering rules, called the Eton Wall Game. Despite continuing chest problems, he also played football vigorously.

on his toes, but at Eton – where he grew to almost his full adult height of 1.9 metres (6 feet 3 inches) – he mainly coasted along.

Eric put little effort into his regular studies but continued to read hungrily. By the age of seventeen he had learned the whole of A. E. Housman's epic poem *A Shropshire Lad* by heart. According to some fellow schoolboys he stood aside from things, 'observing – always observing', and 'speaking with his mouth almost closed, which gave him the appearance of being unemotional or detached'. But future historian Steven Runciman knew that Eric could be sentimental too – especially about the Far East, his birthplace. 'He had hardly known it, but he always used to talk about it. That was where he wanted to go back to.' And that was where, instead of Oxford or Cambridge, he duly went in 1922.

> " *'The regime in College in those days was... fairly rough... The Colleger [King's Scholar] had to expect to be beaten a number of times during his first two years. It was thought to be good for him, and, even if he did not commit an offence, some offence would probably be fathered on him quite without malice and for the good of his bottom and general entertainment.'* "
> Christopher Hollis, a future author and MP, who was at Eton at the same time as Eric

Burmese Days

In 1922 Eric Blair went to Mandalay, Burma (now Myanmar) to train as an officer in the Indian Imperial Police. He got to know the country well – he lived and worked there for five long years, until 1927.

Forging a career

No one quite knows why Eric chose this career. According to his Eton friend Steven Runciman, he was attracted by the independence of the job and the amount of responsibility it carried. Having survived some exams in London in mid-1922, which included a riding test, he became a **probationary** assistant district superintendent of police. When he set sail from Liverpool to Rangoon (Burma's capital) later that year, he was nineteen years old. He might have expected to stay in the job until he was fifty-five, with visits home at five-year intervals.

Eric Blair stands third from the left in this photo of the Police Training School in Mandalay, taken in 1923. 'We keep the peace in India, in our own interest,' said an English character in his first novel, *Burmese Days* (1934), 'but what does all this law and order business boil down to? More banks and more prisons – that's all it means.'

> **"** '[Eric] always looked as if his clothes would never hang on to him properly… You couldn't make him tidy however hard you tried… Whereas I found it very difficult to learn Burmese and Hindustani, it didn't seem to worry him at all… I'm told that before he left Burma, he was able to go into a Hpongyi Kyaung, which is one of those Burmese temples, and converse in very **high-flown** Burmese with the Hpongyis, or priests, and you've got to be able to speak very well to be able to do that.' **"**
>
> Roger Beadon (1969), who worked with Eric in Burma

Little is known about Eric's day-to-day life in Burma after his training in Mandalay. As an assistant superintendent, he was posted to five different districts during his five years, and seems to have been given more and more responsibility by his superiors. In a country of thirteen million people, there was a large native-born police force of 13,000 men – but Eric was one of only 90 Indian Imperial Police officers there. At 21, he was placed in charge of a local force of nearly 200 men at Syriam. In the Twante subdivision in the Hanthawaddy district, he was the head of a police force that was responsible for keeping law and order among 200,000 people.

Burma was a poor country, with a high level of lawlessness, but British officers were mainly involved in **administration**; they rarely had to fight crime on their own. 'You could never understand how awful it is if you hadn't been here,' Eric wrote home to Jacintha Buddicom, soon after he arrived. It is perhaps surprising that he stuck it out for as long as he did, before giving it up to become a writer.

Lasting impressions

As George Orwell, Eric later wrote dismissively of the time he spent in Burma. In 1946, for example, he wrote: 'From a very early age I knew that when I grew up I should be a writer. Between the ages of about seventeen and twenty-four [he was in Burma from the ages of nineteen to twenty-four] I tried to abandon this idea, but I did so with the consciousness that I was outraging my true nature and that sooner or later I should have to settle down and write books.' Yet his experiences in the Far East had a profound effect on the rest of his life. Not only did they give him the material for his novel *Burmese Days*, and for shorter pieces like 'A Hanging' and 'Shooting an Elephant', they deepened his hatred of 'every form of man's **dominion** over man', which had begun at St Cyprian's.

Elisa-Maria Langford-Rae knew Eric in Burma: 'I once remarked to him on the minute care with which he sifted each case, his passion for justice, his dislike about prejudiced remarks about anyone, however lowly, and his sense of utter fairness in his minutest dealings.' This implies that not all British police officers were quite so fair. Eric found the sometimes **racist** attitudes of many Europeans living abroad very different from his own. And he saw how easy it was to acquire a false sense of superiority. He himself got into lazy habits, and allowed himself to be dressed and undressed daily by a Burmese boy servant.

'Shooting an Elephant'

'Shooting an Elephant', a piece first published in 1936, was based on one of Eric's experiences in Burma. It began: 'In Moulmein, in Lower Burma, I was hated by large numbers of people – the only time in my life that I have been important enough for this to happen to me.' Plainly he disliked this, but he also disliked the expectations that the Burmese people had of their British masters. One day an elephant that had been trained to move heavy teak logs strayed into town. It was a docile creature, and doing no harm, but elephants 'on the rampage' were normally shot by policemen. So a large crowd gathered, hoping to see the British policeman 'act like a **sahib**'. They expected him 'to know his own mind and do definite things'. In this case, the definite thing was to kill the harmless elephant. Eric felt himself to be 'an absurd puppet'. He sensed that he was being 'pushed to and fro by the will of those yellow faces behind', and finally, 'solely to avoid looking a fool', he shot the poor beast. 'When the white man turns tyrant,' he concluded, 'it is his own freedom he destroys.'

Four years after leaving Burma, Eric wrote the magazine piece 'A Hanging'. In it, he describes a Hindu convict being escorted across a prison yard to the gallows. When the man sees a puddle, he steps aside to avoid it. 'Till that moment,' the ex-policeman wrote, 'I had never realised what it means to destroy a healthy, conscious man... His brain still remembered, foresaw, reasoned – reasoned even about puddles. He and we were a party of men walking together, seeing, hearing, feeling, understanding the same world; and in two minutes, with a sudden snap, one of us would be gone – one mind less, one world less.'

Burma left a lasting impression on Eric. In his novel *Burmese Days* (1934), he attacked both racist Europeans in Burma and corrupt Burmese officials. According to Roger Beadon, a colleague in Burma, when one of Eric's former bosses read it, 'he went livid and said that if he ever met that young man he was going to horse-whip him'.

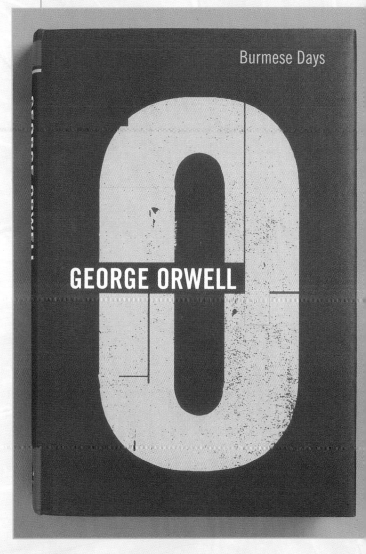

In 1927 Eric's always-fragile health was hit by a bad bout of **dengue fever**. He came home to his family to convalesce and decided not to return to Burma. On 1 January 1928 he left the Indian Imperial Police. Now at last, he believed, the time had come for him to 'settle down and write books'.

Going native in his own country

Few people have ever heard of the writers P. S. Burton, Kenneth Miles or H. Lewis Allways. That is hardly surprising – none of them has ever had a book published. None of them, in fact, ever existed. They were all **pseudonyms** that Eric considered using before he finally settled, in late 1932, on George Orwell.

The first book to appear under this name was *Down and Out in Paris and London* in early 1933. It was a vivid, largely factual account of life among society's poorest classes, much of it based on Eric's own experiences. He had several reasons for not using his own name as author. He simply did not like the sound of 'Eric Blair'; and by the time the book was published, he declared that he was 'not proud of it' – so he was keen to avoid a sense of personal responsibility if it was a total failure! But he also wanted to spare his family any embarrassment.

His father had been baffled and hurt when Eric gave up his job in Burma to try to become a writer. Soon after, when Eric spent time researching the plight of the poor by living among them in the guise of a tramp,

Eric in the late 1920s. According to his younger sister Avril, while he was in Burma he had changed both in looks and manner: 'I suppose being used to a lot of servants in India he'd become – to our minds – untidy. Whenever he smoked a cigarette he threw the end down on the floor – and the match – and expected other people to sweep them up.'

and working as a kitchen dogsbody in a Paris hotel, his father must have thought it quite shameful. So, by hiding behind a pseudonym, Eric hoped that none of his readers would be able to identify him as the son of the 'respectable' ex-colonial administrator living in Southwold.

'Like a cow with a musket'

Eric was no overnight success as an author. He wrote a lot before he had anything published. And fourteen years would pass before he earned as much as he had earned in his last year in Burma. Meanwhile, from 1928 to 1933, he often took other jobs – like teaching or hop picking – to help make ends meet. For some of the time he lived with his family in Southwold, while at other times he stayed in cheap rented rooms in London. For eighteen months, in a quest for inspiration, he even scraped an existence in Paris.

At first he did not even know what he wanted to write. 'He used to sit down at nine o'clock in a little back room [in his parents' home] where there was a table and writing things,' recalled a friend from Southwold, 'and he used to write till twelve. And at twelve o'clock he'd throw everything down and go out and have a beer. Well it didn't matter what he wrote as long as he wrote. He was forcing himself to write. Anything that came into his head he wrote it.'

Unusual tutoring

Richard Peters was one of three boys tutored by Eric in Southwold during 1930. In 1955, Richard remembered 'a tall spindly young man with a great mop of hair waving on top of a huge head, swinging along with loose, effortless strides and a knobbly stick made of some queer Scandinavian wood... He would discuss anything with interest, yet objectively and without **prejudice**... But [the activity] that stands out in my memory most is the making of bombs.' Eric made his own gunpowder – and once seriously frightened the boys' grandmother by blowing up a grassy mound in the garden near the sitting-room window. But he also took the boys on walks to study the herons at Blythburgh or to look for the nests of swans or **plovers** in the estuary of the River Blyth.

Although there was much economic distress in 1930s Britain, Eric at first chose to investigate the plight of tramps rather than the simply poverty-stricken.

While living in London, according to the poet Ruth Pitter, after all the heat of Burma 'he would sometimes warm his hands at a candle before he would start to write. And do you know, he wrote so badly. He had to teach himself writing, he was like a cow with a musket; it was sheer hard grind.' He typed whole novels that never saw the light of day. But from late 1929 he started getting some documentary articles and book reviews published in magazines. One of these articles was 'A Hanging' (see page 17); another was 'The Spike', about one of his early tramping expeditions outside London.

Since 1927 he had been fascinated to know how the working class lived. He wanted to find out if these 'British natives' were as badly treated as those in Burma. So for nights on end he pretended to be a tramp, and made investigations among the poverty-stricken. 'We always argued about this,' said his friend Brenda Salkeld, who in 1930 rejected his proposal of marriage, 'because he said he was getting to know what it was like to be a tramp, but I felt quite certain that just putting on tramp's clothes and walking, does not make you a tramp because you knew you could always get back home.'

Eric becomes George

But Eric kept on tramping, and he recorded his eye-opening findings in the book that became *Down and Out in Paris and London*. By late 1930 he had completed a manuscript, which he then continued to work on, but when he submitted it to two leading London publishers, they rejected it. One of these publishers was the celebrated poet T. S. Eliot of the firm Faber and Faber. Disheartened, Eric gave up on the book. Handing the typescript over to his friend Mabel Fierz, he told her to throw it away, 'but keep the paper-clips'.

Luckily Mabel did no such thing. Instead, without telling Eric, she showed the book to Leonard Moore, a London literary **agent**. Moore contacted Eric with an offer to represent him, and in June 1932 he found him a publisher – Victor Gollancz, a keen **Socialist** who had started up his own successful firm four years earlier. (Gollancz published popular fiction, biographies and **anthologies** which – unusually for the time – he promoted with a great deal of newspaper advertising.) He offered Eric a rather meagre **advance** – even in those days – of just £40 for his book, which then came out in January 1933.

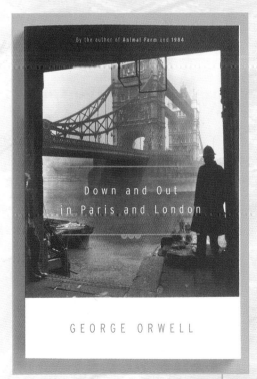

Leonard Moore not only found an English publisher for *Down and Out*, he found an American one too – Harper and Brothers. They published the book in June 1933, again to some favourable reviews, but without selling huge numbers.

Down and Out in Paris and London sold fewer than 3000 copies, but several newspapers gave it good reviews. One compared its eccentric characters to those of an author whom Eric greatly admired, Charles Dickens. In the book, Eric – or George as we may now call him – offered no solution to the problem of poverty. He simply wanted to alter people's perceptions of the poor – and he did so with considerable literary skill, descriptive power and even some flashes of humour. As another journal, *Time and Tide* remarked, 'It is not only George Orwell's experiences that are interesting; George Orwell himself is of interest.'

Keep the Aspidistra Flying

'Writing is bosh,' declared a character called Boris in *Down and Out in Paris and London*. 'There is only one way to make money at writing,

and that is to marry a publisher's daughter.' These may have been Orwell's personal sentiments. In the years from 1933 to 1936 he had three novels published, as well as plenty of journalism, much of it for *New English Weekly*. Although this writing enabled him to build a reputation, it brought him in very little money. So he had to keep up day jobs like school-teaching and working in a bookshop.

Orwell wrote *A Clergyman's Daughter* here, at 36 High Street, Southwold, the Blairs' family home from 1929 until 1939. He was so fond of the region that he named himself after a river that reaches the sea 35 miles from Southwold – the Orwell.

Kay Ekevall, a girlfriend from that time, said in 1984: 'He had a phobia about money... he thought he was terribly poor.' His 'phobia' came out, in fictional form, in his third novel from this period – *Keep The Aspidistra Flying*. He continued to draw on his own experiences in all his fiction. But he found it hard to organize his novels. 'I can write decent passages,' he once told a friend, 'but I can't put them together.' (Some critics have called this a major flaw in his fiction.) He also admitted, 'With me almost any piece of writing has to be done over and over again. I wish I were one of those people who can sit down and fling off a novel in about four days.'

Orwell the squeaker

Orwell would re-read work by his favourite writers to try to fathom the secrets of their success. One of these writers was James Joyce, author of the masterpiece *Ulysses*. 'When I read a book like that then come back to my own work,' Orwell sighed, 'I feel like a **eunuch** who has

22

taken a course in voice
production and can pass
himself off fairly well as a
bass or baritone, but if you
listen closely you can hear the
good old squeak just the
same as ever.' Yet he still
thought that with enough
hard work, and a little luck,
he *could* establish himself as
a major writer.

Orwell in a relatively rare moment of relaxation in 1934. 'I've never known anybody that worked as hard as Eric did,' his brother-in-law Humphrey Dakin remembered in 1970. 'As soon as he'd had his meal and we'd had a bit of a chat on this, that and the other, he'd disappear to his room and you'd hear his typewriter going right through the night.'

Orwell finished his first novel
Burmese Days at the end of
1933. It was very nearly his
last one too. Just before
Christmas he was struck
down by a severe attack of
pneumonia, and was
admitted to Uxbridge Cottage
Hospital. When his family
visited, they found him
delirious and close to death.
He survived, but his mother
then persuaded him to give
up his strenuous teaching job
in Uxbridge, Middlesex.
Instead he returned to Southwold to begin work on another novel.

Orwell was not put off by lukewarm reviews of *Burmese Days*, when it
was published in the USA by Harpers and in Britain by Gollancz. 'I am
sick of the sight of it,' he had told his **agent**. 'Let's hope the next one
will be better.' By the end of 1934 he had finished *A Clergyman's
Daughter*, which Gollancz published in 1935 and Harpers in 1936.
Clearly his publishers were prepared to keep backing him, although
on this novel Orwell was not sure why. 'It was a good idea,' he told his

23

agent, 'but I am afraid I have made a muck of it.' His idea had been to write about a spinster, Dorothy Hare, who scandalizes her father's East Anglian parish when she 'drops out' of refined, middle-class society to experience, at first hand, life in the hopfields of Kent and on the streets of London. Reviews were mixed, sales were low but – at least in Britain – not disastrous. Victor Gollancz was still keen to see what he wrote next.

Art imitating life

Orwell's third novel, *Keep The Aspidistra Flying*, gives some fascinating glimpses of Orwell's own life in 1935 and early 1936, when he wrote it. Like its hero, Gordon Comstock, Orwell was an obscure author with big ambitions. Also like Comstock, Orwell had a day job in a bookshop called Booklover's Corner, in Hampstead, London, where he worked in the afternoons and wrote for the rest of the time in lodgings above it.

All sorts of customers came into Orwell's shop, 'from baronets to bus-conductors'. Some of the vaguer browsers got on his nerves. 'Many of the people who came to us were of the kind who would be a nuisance anywhere but have special opportunities in a bookshop.' But Orwell learned a lot about the book business and what people liked to read. He also got to know Kay Ekevall, who came in to talk about books, and she became his girlfriend. It is possible that Gordon's girlfriend Rosemary in *Aspidistra* is based a little on her. 'He was a very self-sufficient person,' Kay recalled in 1984. 'He could cook and mend his clothes and all that sort of thing. And I admired him for that a lot.'

In the novel Gordon rants about the corrupt world around him, where money and power count for far more than high art. He leaves a career in advertising ('the rattling of a stick inside a swill-bucket') to try to write great poetry. But unable to meet his own lofty standards, he loses faith and returns to advertising, where he helps to launch a new foot deodorant. Gordon despises himself for selling out – for finally wanting to make a

In 1997 *Keep the Aspidistra Flying* was turned into a film. It was not a great success. Some of the reviews were even worse than those received by Orwell himself when the book was published in 1936!

little money, put an aspidistra plant in the front window and enjoy home comforts like so many other people.

The novel was published in Britain in April 1936. (Orwell's American publishers did not want it – and it appeared in the USA only after his death.) Out of its first printing of 3000, only 2194 copies were sold.

A happy vicar?
Orwell wrote these verses in 1935, reflecting on how, once upon a time, he might have lived in an 'aspidistra' world of his own:

> 'A happy vicar I might have been
> Two hundred years ago,
> To preach upon eternal doom
> And watch my walnuts grow;
>
> 'But born alas, in an evil time,
> I missed that pleasant haven,
> For the hair has grown on my upper lip
> And the clergy are all clean-shaven.'

Some of the reviews were very critical. Even his old school friend Cyril Connolly wrote in the *New Statesman* that he found it inferior to *Burmese Days*. Orwell was hardly surprised. He himself dismissed it in the same way he had *A Clergyman's Daughter*, calling it 'a silly **potboiler**'. But unlike Gordon, he did not intend to give up his art.

Making the grade with Eileen

On 9 June 1936, at the age of 33, Orwell got married – not to Kay Ekevall, but to Eileen O'Shaughnessy. He had met her at a party in March 1935, and been attracted by her good looks, dry wit and great intelligence. A graduate of Oxford University she was now, at 29, studying for a postgraduate diploma in educational pyschology. Orwell proposed soon after meeting her.

Some people thought Orwell would prove a difficult man to live with. 'You are taking on something!' one person said privately to Eileen at the wedding – and that was Orwell's own mother! But they would stay together until Eileen's early death in 1945 at just 39 years of age, and they generally gave the impression of being happily married. Eileen was a keen and helpful reader of her husband's **work-in-progress** and sometimes – especially with *Animal Farm* (see pages 44–45) – she could influence the way it turned out.

Eileen in 1938. Born in the north-east of England, she came from a gifted family. Her brother, Laurence, who died in World War II in 1940, was one of Britain's leading experts on **tuberculosis** – the disease that would kill Orwell in 1950.

The Road to Wigan Pier

In 1946 Orwell looked back at his work over the past decade. After writing *Keep The Aspidistra Flying*, it was clear to him that his career had taken a new direction. 'My starting point,' he wrote, referring to all his books since then, 'is always a feeling of **partisanship**, a sense of injustice. When I sit down to write a book, I do not say to myself, "I am going to produce a work of art." I write it because there is some lie that I want to expose, some fact to which I want to draw attention, and my initial concern is to get a hearing.'

These are interesting comments. There is little doubt that the 'missing element' in Orwell's writing, before 1936, was a strong political point of view. But this does not mean that after 1936 his books cannot be called 'works of art'. Far from it. His later books and essays show him to be a very great literary artist indeed. Having discovered what he really needed to write about, Orwell's unique gifts as a writer then seemed to flower as well.

'A very serious mess'

'It hardly needs pointing out,' wrote Orwell in 1937, 'that we are in a very serious mess.' He meant 'we' in a large sense. The world of the mid-1930s was not a comfortable place in which to live. If Orwell was seeking 'a sense of injustice' to motivate his writing, he did not have far to look. The rise of aggressive, unprincipled **Fascist** dictators in Europe was threatening to cause another appalling conflict like World War I had, two decades earlier. Closer to home, huge numbers of British working people were suffering poverty and hardship – the effects of a worldwide **Great Depression**. (In Britain, nearly three million men became unemployed; that meant roughly one worker in five was without a job, with Wales and the north of England the hardest hit.) But beneath this economic distress lay the deeper 'injustice' of the British class system.

Orwell himself was born into the relatively privileged middle class. Millions of other Britons were condemned to lead hard and unrewarding lives just because they happened to be members of the 'working class'. The more Orwell thought about this, the more unjust it

Victor Gollancz, who published all but one of Orwell's books in the 1930s. An article about Gollancz in the *News Chronicle* of 1932 said he could read a 75,000 word manuscript in 45 minutes! Passionate about politics, he was a deeply committed Socialist.

seemed, and the keener he became to change things, perhaps in a **socialist** way. As he later wrote in *The Lion and the Unicorn* (see page 41), all the people in the country made up a family – 'a family with the wrong members in control'.

Orwell travels north

Someone else who hated social injustice was Orwell's British publisher, Victor Gollancz. After Orwell finished *Aspidistra*, Gollancz suggested that he might now travel around the depressed north of England, gathering material for a new non-fiction book about the plight of the unemployed. Since he also offered him a very large **advance** of £500, Orwell thought this was a fine idea!

So for two months in early 1936, Orwell researched the lives of jobless and working people in Wigan, Liverpool, Sheffield and Barnsley – living in their homes, visiting their workplaces, finding out about their attitudes. Shocked and pained by his research, Orwell had finally found a subject worthy of his writing skills. As he made clear in the absorbing book he then wrote, *The Road to Wigan Pier*, human life in the north was held far too cheaply. When, for example, a coal miner was killed doing his incredibly dangerous job, a **shilling** was taken out of all the other miners' wages that week, to be put into a fund for the widow. This happened so often that the employers used a rubber stamp to print 'Death stoppage' on the miners' pay checks. It was as if they took death for granted.

Orwell did not call for any political party – Socialist or otherwise – to abolish poverty 'from above'. (He said writers must be free to form their own opinions, so they could not be *loyal* members of a political party.) Rather, he wanted 'all people with small, insecure incomes... to fight on the same side... This means that the smallholder has got to ally himself with the factory-hand, the typist with the coal miner, the schoolmaster with the garage mechanic. There is some hope of getting them to do so if they can be made to understand where their interest lies.' *The Road to Wigan Pier* was his attempt to help in that cause.

The book certainly reached more readers than any of his previous publications. Gollancz published a cut-price **Left Book Club** edition of over 40,000 copies, then reissued it twice more. It provided food for thought for many, although some **left-wing** reviewers and readers found his account too personal, and not factual enough. They criticized him for being 'a disillusioned little middle-class boy' writing on a 'subject that he does not understand'. Richard Rees, however, later called the book 'a sensation... Besides revealing what [Orwell] had seen in the mining towns of the north, he began to reveal his true self.'

> "
> *'As [the train] moved slowly through the outskirts of the town [Wigan] we passed row after row of little grey slum houses... At the back of one of the houses a young woman was kneeling on the stones, poking a stick up the leaden waste-pipe which ran from the sink inside and which I suppose was blocked. I had time to see everything about her – her sacking apron, her clumsy clogs, her arms reddened by the cold. She looked up as the train passed, and I was almost near enough to catch her eye... It struck me then that we are mistaken when we say that "It isn't the same for them as it would be for us," and that people bred in the slums can imagine nothing but the slums... She knew well enough what was happening to her – understood as well as I did how dreadful a destiny it was to be kneeling there in the bitter cold, on the slimy stones of a slum backyard, poking a stick up a foul drainpipe.'*
> From George Orwell's *The Road to Wigan Pier* (1937)

A top-hatted Eton schoolboy ignores less privileged children in 1937. Orwell detested such clear class distinction.

George the grocer

When Orwell came back from the north, he did not return to the Hampstead bookshop. Instead he wrote *Wigan Pier* in a tiny village called Wallington in Hertfordshire, 56 kilometres (35 miles) north of London. That was where he had taken up a new day job. Rather surprisingly for a fiercely political writer, he had become a local shopkeeper – mainly selling sweets to children.

'The Stores' was in a bad way when Orwell took it over. There was no electricity, no indoor toilet and no hot tap water. But he was never afraid of hard manual work, and soon he got the place into shape – and later even raised some chickens, ducks and goats outside. Before long he was selling enough groceries each week to cover his rent. With the help of Eileen, he took this work seriously – without them, there would have been no village shop at all. But they opened only in the afternoons; in the mornings Orwell wrote.

The first fight with Fascism

'I think what changed Eric completely was the Spanish War,' said Orwell's brother-in-law Humphrey Dakin in an interview in 1970. 'He went [to fight in Spain] and he learnt a lot. And he came back a changed man. He used to say sometimes that he wished he'd been in the war, the 1914–18 war... Perhaps the Spanish War filled in a gap in his experience.'

The year 1936 was one of contrasts for Orwell. First he spent two months in the cramped and crowded towns of the poverty-stricken north; then he and his new wife virtually isolated themselves in a village shop; and he ended the year by volunteering to fight for **left-wing** forces in the Spanish Civil War. It might seem strange that a middle-class Englishman should choose to fight alongside the working men of another country. But although Orwell had strong feelings for England, he also cared deeply about injustices abroad. Nor was he alone in believing that the fight against **Fascism** was an international struggle.

The Spanish Civil War, 1936–39

In 1931 the Spanish monarchy was replaced by a **republic**. By 1936 some sections of the Spanish population believed that the Republic's elected government was too left-wing. In these circumstances, **a right-wing** general, Francisco Franco, led a Fascist revolt against the Popular Front government. Franco's forces, called the Nationalists, were supported by Fascist Italy and Nazi Germany. They seized power in the south and north-west of Spain, but workers' **militias** held them off in Madrid and Barcelona. These 'Republican' forces were aided by the **Communist** government of the **USSR**, and also by volunteers from many other countries. The war went on until 1939, when the Nationalists finally took Madrid and Barcelona. General Franco then set up a **dictatorship** and remained in power until his death in 1975.

On his way to the front, Orwell met Czechs, Frenchmen and men of other nationalities – all travelling to Spain to show **solidarity** with their Spanish comrades. He would remain in Spain for six months, spending 115 days on the Aragon front. There he would prove to be a capable soldier – and would almost lose his life.

'A plague of initials'

When Orwell left for Spain at Christmas time in 1936, his aim was to help the Republicans by observing the war and writing truthfully about it. He believed that his poor health would stop him from being an effective soldier. He did finally write a book about the war – *Homage to Catalonia* was published in Britain in April 1938 – but on 30 December 1936 in Barcelona he enlisted in the militia of the POUM (Workers' Party of **Marxist** Unification).

In early January 1937 he went to serve at the front line at Alcubierre. Later that month, by now promoted to *cabo* (corporal), he switched to a unit of the Independent Labour Party that had arrived from England to serve with the POUM militia on the Aragon front. In his book *Homage to Catalonia*, Orwell described how confused he was by all the groups or 'factions' that made up the Republican side. There was 'a kaleidoscope of political parties and trade unions, with their tiresome names – PSUC, POUM, FAI, CNT, UGT, JCI, JSU, AIT… It looked at first sight as though Spain were suffering from a plague of initials.' And some of these factions were keener to dispute among themselves than to resist the Fascist threat. 'I thought it idiotic that people fighting for their lives should *have* separate parties,' Orwell wrote. 'My attitude always was, "Why can't we drop all this political nonsense and get on with the war?"'

Orwell himself not only got on with the war, he got on with his writing at the same time. He made light of the Fascists' artillery attacks: 'The Fascist guns were of the same make and calibre as our own, and the unexploded shells were often reconditioned and fired back. There was said to be one old shell with a nickname of its own which travelled daily to and fro, never exploding.'

> **"** '[Orwell] came striding towards me – all 6 foot 3 of him – dressed in a grotesque mixture of clothing – corduroy riding breeches, khaki **puttees** and huge boots caked with mud, a yellow pigskin jerkin, a chocolate-coloured balaclava helmet with a knitted khaki scarf of immeasurable length wrapped round and round his neck and face up to his ears, an old-fashioned German rifle over his shoulder and two hand-grenades hanging from his belt.' **"**
> Robert Edwards (1970), who fought with Orwell in Spain

John Donovan, an Irishman, shared a dugout with Orwell at Monte Trazo. 'Orwell always wanted to be in action,' he remembered, 'he never wanted to lie down and take things easy, but wanted always to carry on.' But he was also 'always writing. In the daytime he used to sit outside the dugout writing, and in the evenings he used to write by candlelight.' Orwell was not, however, destined to take this detailed war-diary back to England with him.

Orwell is the tall man at the centre of this photo taken on the Aragon front in March 1937. The woman kneeling in front of him is his wife Eileen. In February she too arrived in Barcelona, to help the Republican war effort.

A miraculous escape

By 20 May 1937, Orwell had risen to the rank of an officer, as a lieutenant. But at first light that day, his war came to an abrupt end. Leaving the dugout to relieve one of his men who was standing on guard, he looked out over the protective wall of sandbags and was shot in the throat from 183 metres (200 yards) by a Fascist sniper.

Still conscious, he was rushed to a small hospital at Monflorite, then on to another hospital at Sietamo, before he could be moved to a **sanatorium** outside Barcelona where he convalesced for two weeks. He recovered remarkably quickly. Doctors later told him the bullet had missed an artery by 'about a millimetre'. That was how close he came to certain death. But the wound left him unfit for service. 'Declared useless', it said on his medical discharge.

With Eileen, he prepared to return to England. That was not as simple as it sounded. As in-fighting between the left-wing factions increased, on 16 June the Republican government outlawed the POUM and threw its leaders into prison. In his absence, Orwell's own room in Barcelona was ransacked by plain-clothes policemen. They took as 'evidence' his books, letters and diaries (as well as a bundle of his dirty washing!), and would have arrested him if he had not hidden out on the streets for a few days before escaping into France.

Pablo Picasso's *Guernica* was inspired by the horrific bombing campaigns of the Spanish Civil War.

Orwell's account of his experiences in the Spanish region of Catalonia is now seen as a classic of personal political writing. Although the Socialist revolution in Spain failed, Orwell never forgot that 'for several months large blocks of people believed that all men are equal and were able to act on their belief. The result was a feeling of liberation and hope' – and it led him to write an optimistic book.

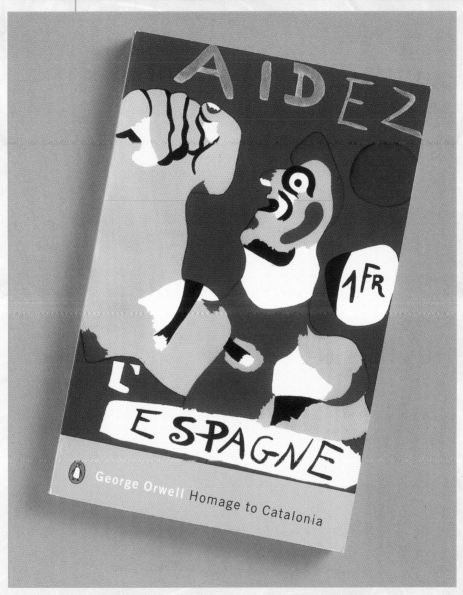

He came home knowing that in the world of political warfare, it was sometimes easier to know what you were fighting against than to know who you were fighting with. But he also returned with a new certainty. 'At last,' he told Cyril Connolly, '[I] really believe in **Socialism**, which I never did before.'

A new publisher

Back at The Stores in Wallington, Orwell wrote *Homage to Catalonia* between July 1937 and January 1938. On arriving in Barcelona, he had been impressed by what looked like a real 'workers' state'. There was an atmosphere of people pulling together in a spirit of equality – even the waiters 'looked you in the face and treated you as an equal'. But by the time he left, he had lost faith in the Republican government. By imprisoning people without trial and preventing freedom of speech, it seemed to be Fascist itself in all but name.

In his book, Orwell made many criticisms of the Communists in Spain, and queried the motives of the USSR's dictator Joseph Stalin for getting involved. He sensed that Stalin's desire for power and influence in Europe was hardly different from that of right-wing leaders like Germany's Adolf Hitler. Views like these were not acceptable to many British left-wingers. They believed that Stalin and the Communists offered the greatest hope of holding back the tide of Fascism, not only in Spain but elsewhere in Europe too. Victor Gollancz, a committed Communist, thus wanted nothing to do with Orwell's book.

Luckily for Orwell, other publishers were more politically broad-minded. Fredric Warburg, a director of Secker and Warburg, was only too keen to put *Homage to Catalonia* into print. His firm was at that time small, but Orwell's later books would finally help to make it very big. *Homage to Catalonia*, however, did not get the new relationship off to a good start. The book received a number of bad reviews, and the 1250 copies printed did not all sell until after Orwell's death in 1950, twelve years later.

As Orwell moved on to his next writing project he was, as his brother-in-law had pointed out, a changed man. His experiences in Spain had filled him with 'not less but more belief in the decency of human beings'. The idealism and heroism of ordinary individuals made a lasting impression on him. But he had also seen what evils could arise when large numbers of people blindly follow a political **creed** – whether left-wing or right-wing. And he would spend the last twelve years of his life alerting his readers to this danger.

Coming Up For Air

The period from 1938 to 1940 was not a happy one for Orwell. After coughing up large amounts of blood, he had to spend five and a half months of 1938 in a Kent **sanatorium**. His doctors could not diagnose **tuberculosis**, although he was repeatedly tested for it. He was allowed to do almost no writing, then advised to spend the winter in a warmer climate than England's. This was financially impossible for Orwell, until an admirer of his work stepped in. Through mutual friends, the novelist L. H. Myers **anonymously** offered him and Eileen £300 to finance a stay abroad. Orwell accepted the cash, but only as a loan, which he dutifully paid back when he could – eight years later.

Making the most of Morocco

Orwell and Eileen spent six months from September 1938 in Morocco. 'A beastly dull country,' Orwell complained, 'no forests and literally no wild animals.' It is surprising that he saw anything at all of this part of North Africa, since he was working so hard on another book.

Orwell writing in Marrakech in 1939. Despite his health problems, he kept on smoking a particularly strong, black tobacco.

In late 1937, Orwell had told his **agent** he had an idea for a new novel: 'it will be about a man who is having a holiday and trying to make a temporary escape from responsibility, public and private. The title I thought of is *Coming Up For Air*.' He began work on it in Morocco, and on his return to London in March 1939 he brought with him the finished manuscript. Within three months it had been published – once again by Victor Gollancz, who by contract still had first refusal on Orwell's books, even though he had declined to publish *Homage to Catalonia*.

Coming Up For Air fared rather better than Orwell's earlier novels. Some of its reviews were very good, and the book sold 3000 copies. Written in the first person, it tells the story of George 'Fatty' Bowling, a middle-aged insurance salesman who feels badly out of step with the late-1930s world. Both Georges – Bowling and Orwell – were writing on the eve of World War II, a time of great tension, fear and uncertainty. In the novel, George Bowling revisits the places where he spent a happy boyhood – in the Thames Valley, where Orwell himself grew up. He wants to take a last look at the old landmarks before enemy bombers destroy them forever, but he finds everything changed already. All he has to console him are memories.

'Things look rather black'

When war broke out in September 1939, Orwell was eager to serve his country. Not surprisingly, he was rejected by the army as medically unfit, but for a while he would not take no for an answer. The War Office had more trouble keeping him out of the army, remarked the poet Paul Potts, than it did in getting hundreds of other to join. Eileen took a clerical job at Whitehall in London to help the war effort. That meant she had to live in London with her sister-in-law during the week, coming home to Wallington only at weekends.

Deeply frustrated, Orwell pottered on at The Stores, working as a journalist and also writing three long essays: 'Inside the Whale' (see page 5), 'Charles Dickens' and 'Boys' Weeklies'. When he submitted

> " ... "
>
> *'I was walking westward up the Strand, and though it was coldish I went slowly to get the pleasure of my cigar. The usual crowd that you can hardly fight your way through was streaming up the pavement, all of them with that insane fixed expression on their faces that people have in London streets, and there was the usual jam of traffic with the great red buses nosing their way between the cars, and the engines roaring and horns tooting... This kind of prophetic feeling... keeps coming over me nowadays, the feeling that war's just round the corner and that war's the end of all things... I looked at the dumb-bell faces streaming past. Like turkeys in November, I thought. Not a notion of what's coming to them. It was as if I'd got X-rays in my eyes and could see the skeletons walking.'*
>
> From Orwell's *Coming Up For Air* (1939)

the essays to Gollancz, the publisher agreed to put them out in a single short book entitled *Inside the Whale*, which went on sale in March 1940. But he paid Orwell an **advance** of just £30, the lowest of his entire writing career. Both men knew that books of essays seldom became bestsellers.

Orwell had reached a very low point – unwanted by his country, spending more time apart from his wife than with her, seen by some people as a good writer but apparently unable to reach a wide readership. To add to his troubles, his father had died of cancer at the age of 82, just before the war began. Orwell was with him at the end, but the older man – so disappointed that his son had given up his career in Burma – never saw him win major success as a writer.

Orwell now planned out a huge new novel, a kind of saga with the working title *The Quick and the Dead*. He told his agent that it would have to be published in three parts. But he seems never to have got started on it. 'I can't write with this sort of business [the war] going on,' he wrote in his diary, 'and in a few months there is going to be such a severe paper shortage that very few books will be published. In any case I feel that literature as we have known it is coming to an end. Things look rather black at the moment.'

Four legs good, two legs bad

London was not a good place to be in late 1940. This was when the city was subjected to appallingly heavy air raids by German bombers – just as George Bowling had foreseen in *Coming Up For Air*. Children were **evacuated** to relatively safe parts of the country; others with no reason to stay moved out too. Orwell, being Orwell, felt bound to go the other way. In May 1940, he joined Eileen in central London and remained there for the war's duration.

'He felt enormously at home in the **Blitz**,' Cyril Connolly believed, 'the bravery, the rubble, the shortages, the homeless, the signs of revolutionary temper [spirit].' For years he lived close to death – and in June 1944, he almost suffered a serious loss of another kind. A V-1 flying bomb landed in his and Eileen's street, ruining their flat beyond repair. Salvaging what he could from the rubble, he was relieved to find the complete crumpled typescript of his short new novel. Just over a year later, it would be published – as *Animal Farm*.

Sergeant and scribe

Orwell never managed to serve his country as a soldier, but for three years in London he was a keen and energetic member of the **Home Guard**, later remembered as 'Dad's Army'. He was made a sergeant in the 5th London Battalion, and this gave him an opportunity to resume a favourite boyhood pastime – making his own explosives. He also wrote for a number of journals and newspapers, including the *Observer*, *Tribune* and *Horizon*. Between 1940 and 1946, *Horizon* published some of his best essays. These ranged from 'The Art of Donald McGill', about 'rude' seaside postcards, to the original and thought-provoking 'Politics and the English Language' (see page 48).

For the **left-wing** *Tribune* he supplied a weekly column called 'As I Please'. In it, he wrote about everyday subjects like wild flowers, books, or church architecture, but also discussed matters like censorship, patriotism, his mistrust of intellectuals, and the importance of values like decency and individuality. His writing, according to his friend George Woodcock, was a continuation of his daily life and conversation, reflecting his 'intense interest in the concrete aspects of living'. His clear, simple style was both 'conversational' and technically very precise – an unusual combination in the 1940s. He could also write both humorously and quite beautifully. This all helped in his aim 'to make political writing into an art', and won him a lasting reputation as a journalist with high ideals and a common touch.

This was Orwell's membership card of the National Union of Journalists, from 1943. His shirt-collar is in a bad state, and people often remarked on his scruffy appearance.

A defensive patriot

In the autumn of 1940 Orwell quickly wrote a short non-fiction book, *The Lion and the Unicorn*. It sold more than 12,000 copies. Its publisher, Fredric Warburg, guessed that at least 50,000 people read it – since during wartime, when books were in short supply, they were quickly passed from hand to hand.

It was more like an extended essay than a book – but still it packed a lot of power. In it, Orwell called England 'a family with the wrong members in control… one in which the young are generally thwarted and most of the power is in the hands of irresponsible uncles and bedridden aunts.' Calling for a **Socialist** revolution to 'set the English people free', he listed some changes he wanted to see, including the **nationalization** of major industries, the setting up of a classless education system and a closing of the gap between the incomes of the rich and poor. This would 'transform the nation from top to bottom', yet England would still recognizably be England.

This last point was vital for Orwell. Unlike many left-wingers, who had a more international outlook, Orwell did not despise patriotism. In the words of his friend, *Observer* editor David Astor, he was a defensive patriot, not an aggressive one. Orwell had loved the English landscape from boyhood, he was fascinated by English history, and he had come to respect the English 'national character', with all its quirky customs and habits. (He always wrote and spoke about 'England', not 'Britain'.) His biographer Bernard Crick called him 'a revolutionary in love with the past'. Now, even as the war raged, he wanted to see a very English revolution begin, based on common sense and decency.

Orwell speaks to India

From 1941 until 1943, Orwell did not just write and serve the Home Guard. For the first time since leaving Burma, he also took on a job for the government. This time, at an annual salary of £640, he worked for the BBC Eastern Service as a Talks Producer. From 9.30 till 6.15 each weekday, plus three hours every Saturday, he had to write and make broadcasts to radio listeners in India.

This was a way of reminding the Indian people that their support for Britain in the war mattered very much. (India had an army of over two million men.) Some of the programmes were about cultural matters, some were news commentaries. Orwell worked diligently, but his heart was not in this task. And although India had a population of nearly 300 million, only about 150,000 people had the right radio sets to pick up transmissions from London. He later regarded his two years at the BBC as a waste of time. But his experience of working for such a

Orwell (standing on the left) helps to organize a wartime BBC broadcast to India. The man below him is T. S. Eliot, the famous poet who, as a director of the publishers Faber and Faber, had turned down at least two of Orwell's books.

Helping the Cause

In 1943 Orwell was made the literary editor of the *Tribune*. (Its managing editor, Jon Kimche, knew Orwell since he had once worked with him at Booklover's Corner [see page 24].) In this role Orwell had to **commission** pieces of writing by other authors. He asked the author John Morris to write some book reviews for the **Socialist** journal, which he did. 'Happening one day to meet him in the street,' Morris recalled in 1950, 'I took advantage of the occasion to remind him that I had not been paid. "Oh," he said, smiling rather **sardonically**, "we don't pay for reviews, you know; it's all for the Cause!"' Orwell clearly felt a great commitment to this working-class cause. Once he took Morris to a pub. When Morris asked for 'beer', Orwell snorted that a working-class person would never ask for 'a glass of beer' but 'a pint of bitter'. 'I don't happen to be a working-class person,' Morris pointed out. 'No,' Orwell replied, 'but there's no need to boast about it.'

large organization, and in producing a kind of **propaganda**, would later provide valuable material for his last novel, *Nineteen Eighty-Four*.

Soon after Orwell left the BBC, his life changed even more significantly. Unable to have children of their own, he and Eileen adopted a baby

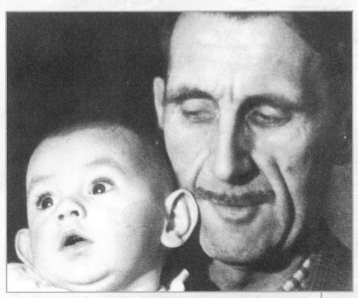

boy, whom they named Richard Horatio Blair. They were both delighted with him, and Eileen gave up a job at the Ministry of Food to become a full-time mother. She had also been helping Orwell with his new book, *Animal Farm*.

Orwell with his beloved adopted son Richard in London.

'All animals are equal'

Animal Farm transformed Orwell's career and ensured his lasting reputation. Published in Britain in August 1945, it sold over 25,000 hardback copies in the first five years. In the USA it was published a year later, but by 1950 its sales had reached a staggering 590,000. It has continued to sell ever since – and in the year 2000 it was translated into its 68th language!

The book is a short, highly political fable. In 1937, Orwell had returned from the Spanish Civil War disillusioned by the intervention of **Communist** Russia under Joseph Stalin. He had also deplored the turn that events had taken inside the **USSR** itself. In his view, the **Russian Revolution** had now been betrayed; the USSR's new rulers were little better than those who had been overthrown in 1917. So he decided to 'expose the Soviet myth', in a story that could easily be understood by almost anyone. How could he do this?

'The actual details of the story did not come to me for some time,' he later wrote, 'until one day (I was then living in a small village) I saw a little boy, perhaps ten years old, driving a huge cart-horse along a narrow path, whipping it whenever it tried to turn. It struck me that if only such animals became aware of their strength we should have no power over them, and that men exploit animals in much the same way as the rich exploit the **proletariat**.' Always a lover of nature and wildlife, Orwell quickly wrote his story as a fable.

In the novel, the animals at 'Manor Farm' rise up in revolt against their human masters and drive them out. For a brief time all goes well. The revolutionaries, declaring 'All animals are equal', run the farm in harmony. But then, as in Communist Russia, some grab more and more power for themselves. In the USSR, it was Stalin and his henchmen. At Animal Farm it is the pigs. 'All animals are equal,' they announce, 'but some animals are more equal than others.' And in the end the pigs become almost indistinguishable from the farm's old human masters. It is an ingenious, funny, wise and powerful book. But when Orwell wrote it – between November 1943 and February 1944 – Stalin's USSR was fighting alongside Britain in World War II. Many

Old Major's rallying cry

Animal Farm begins with a highly respected prize boar, Old Major, addressing the animals of Manor Farm. Urging them to rise up in revolt against humankind, he says, 'Whatever goes upon two legs is an enemy. Whatever goes upon four legs, or has wings, is a friend. And remember also that in fighting against Man, you must not come to resemble him. Even when you have conquered him, do not adopt his vices. No animal must ever live in a house, or sleep in a bed, or wear clothes, or drink alcohol, or smoke tobacco, or touch money, or engage in trade. All the habits of Man are evil. And above all, no animal must ever tyrannize over his own kind. Weak or strong, clever or simple, we are all brothers. No animal must ever kill another animal. All animals are equal.'

publishers, including Victor Gollancz, thus refused to publish it, for fear of offending a vital ally. But again, as with *Homage to Catalonia*, Fredric Warburg took the book on. Even so, it was not published until just after the war, due to a paper shortage.

Animal Farm was not fully understood at the time of its publication. Some readers believed it was a **right-wing** attack on any attempt by working people to improve their lives through revolution. Today it is appreciated as a true classic. The critic Malcolm Bradbury called it 'one of the great modern political **allegories**… a fundamental modern myth'. The moral of the story is that a revolution can work only if the people stay alert and are prepared to 'chuck out' their leaders when the time comes. If they cannot, the future is bleak indeed, as Orwell went on to show in his next and last book.

A scene from the cartoon version of *Animal Farm*, which was made in 1955. Like the book, the film can be enjoyed on several different levels.

The Last Man in Europe

By the time *Animal Farm* was published, Orwell was a single man again. On 29 March 1945 Eileen, who had been in poor health for some time, went into hospital for a **hysterectomy** operation. She died of a heart attack on the operating table. Orwell was in Europe at the time, observing the last stages of the war and reporting on them for the *Observer*. In a stunned state, he hurried home. He missed his wife greatly. Over the next year, possibly as a response to her loss, he sank himself in his work, writing over 130 reviews and articles and publishing a volume of *Critical Essays* in February 1946.

With Eileen gone, Orwell's friends expected him to give up Richard. But he was determined to keep his son, while accepting that he needed a nurse-housekeeper to help him out. The woman he found was 28-year-old Susan Watson, a divorcee with a child of her own. Before employing her, he took her out to dinner at a smart London restaurant for a bizarre test of her suitability.

'George said he had to leave me for a minute,' she remembered in 1983, and 'would I order two drinks. Then he went to stand behind a pillar. I ordered the drinks, and as soon as the waiter had brought them, he emerged. Later he told me that he considered waiters to be very good judges of character, so because I had been served quickly, I had earned the waiter's seal of approval. It seemed to me an unusual way to engage a nurse.' But for a year, before Orwell's younger sister Avril took over her duties, the arrangement worked very well.

The writer in retreat

Orwell did not just have to deal with domestic demands on his time. After the impact of *Animal Farm*, political and literary groups clamoured for him to speak to their meetings, the BBC pressed him for more scripts, and newspaper and journal editors were keener than ever to put his words into print. 'I pine to get free of it all,' he complained to a friend, 'and have some time to think again.' He had striven for so long to be a successful author, but now that he had achieved his ambition, he found he did not enjoy the life of a celebrity.

Orwell worked here, at 'Barnhill' on Jura, on his last novel *Nineteen Eighty-Four*. He found the island very beautiful, despite almost constant rain, and he could also fish, hunt, garden and make minor repairs around the house to his heart's content.

Nor did he rest on his laurels. There were still novels he needed to write, and he knew that with such poor health, he was unlikely to live for much longer.

His friend David Astor suggested a place where Orwell could take breaks from his life in the city: the remote Scottish island of Jura. It was two days' journey from London, and a large farmhouse called 'Barnhill' was available to rent there. Orwell jumped at the chance. From mid-1946 until the summer of 1948, he not only took holidays at the Jura cottage, it almost became his home.

'It's all about the future'

Orwell did not like to talk about his books until he had written them. Fredric Warburg knew that he was writing a novel on Jura. But when he asked what it was about, Orwell would only reply, 'It's all about the future'. Its title at this point was *The Last Man in Europe*. Orwell began it in August 1945 (although he had first thought about in 1943 while the war was still raging) and finished the first draft just over a year later. The second draft took him from May until November 1947, then he typed up a 'clean' final version just before Christmas.

Words matter

In his 1946 essay, 'Politics and the English Language', Orwell argued that writers had a moral duty to think clear thoughts and write in clear words. Most political language, he wrote, 'is designed to makes lies sound truthful… and to give an appearance of solidity to pure wind'. He himself always tried hard to write simply, honestly and with originality. But so much political prose seemed to him to consist 'less and less of words chosen for the sake of their meaning, and more of *phrases* tacked together like the sections of a prefabricated hen-house'. In *Nineteen Eighty-Four*, Orwell went on to show how a corrupt government could actually create a language – 'Newspeak' – with so few real words in it that its speakers lost their ability to frame vital thoughts and ideas.

He had never devoted so much time and concentration to a novel. As a result, the story is wonderfully rounded, and has a clearer sense of direction than most of his other fiction. Its hero, Winston Smith, lives in a shabby London flat in an England that is part of a new **totalitarian** state called Oceania. Oceania is constantly at war with either Eurasia or Eastasia, the world's two other superpowers. Winston's job at the 'Ministry of Truth' is to rewrite history in accordance with the official line of the ruling elite, the Party. Outraged by the immorality of this elite, and the brutality and secrecy of its rule, Winston rebels by entering into a forbidden love affair with the like-minded Julia. But when they then try to contact an underground resistance group, they are arrested, tortured into betraying each other, and finally brainwashed into 'loving' the Party leader, known only as 'Big Brother'.

The book painted a dismal view of the shape of things to come. 'If you want a picture of the future,' Orwell wrote, 'imagine a boot stamping on a human face – for ever.' He had been deeply disturbed by the methods and ideology of Stalin in the USSR and Hitler in Germany. But he set his book in Britain, he claimed, to emphasize 'that totalitarianism, *if not fought against*, could triumph anywhere.' The abuse of power was a universal danger in the post-1945 world.

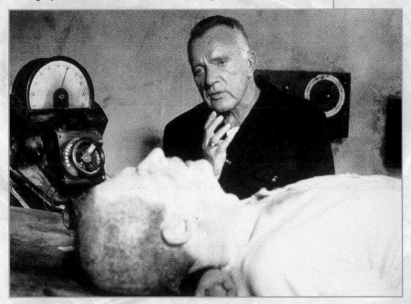

Two plus two equals five

The high-ranking Party official who tortures Winston Smith in *Nineteen Eighty-Four* is called O'Brien. This is one way that he tries to 're-educate' the rebel Winston, whose body has been clamped to a pain-inducing rack:

> '"Do you remember," he [O'Brien] went on, "writing in your diary, *Freedom is the freedom to say that two plus two make four?*"
> "Yes," said Winston.
> O'Brien held up his left hand, its back towards Winston, with the thumb hidden and the four fingers extended.
> "How many fingers am I holding up, Winston?"
> "Four."
> "And if the Party says that it is not four but five then how many?"
> "Four"...
> At that point O'Brien sent appalling spasms of pain into Winston's body, and repeatedly asked him "How many fingers?", until finally the victim cried out:
> "Four! Five! Four! Anything you like. Only stop it, stop the pain!"'

British designers have used great ingenuity in their covers for *Nineteen Eighty-Four*. Several feature eye motifs, to underline the Party slogan in Orwell's novel: 'Big Brother is Watching You.'

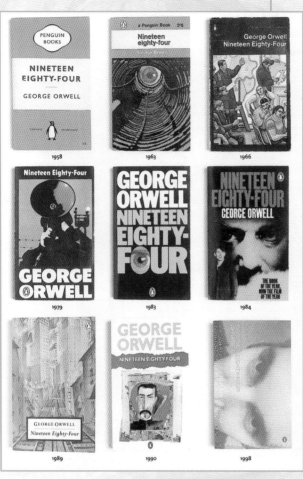

1958

1963

1966

1979

1983

1984

1989

1990

1998

Both Warburg in the UK, and the US publishers Harcourt, Brace, were delighted with this chilling, **apocalyptic** yet often darkly humorous book. At Warburg's suggestion, the title was changed to *Nineteen Eighty-Four* (the simple result of swapping the last two digits of the year they were then living in: 1948). It was published in both countries in June 1949 and was an immediate bestseller. A year later it had sold nearly 50,000 copies in Britain and 170,000 in the USA (with a further 190,000 sales in a special 'Book-of-the-Month Club' edition). Ever since, it has continued to be bought and read all over the world.

As with *Animal Farm*, some reviewers of *Nineteen Eighty-Four* believed Orwell was attacking **left-wing** politics, or even the British Labour Party. But many greeted the novel as a modern classic. In the USA, Lionel Trilling called it 'profound, terrifying, and wholly fascinating'. In Britain the writer V. S. Pritchett described it as 'a book that goes through the reader like an east wind, cracking the skin, opening the sores'. Even today, few can deny its power and vividness.

A new lease of life?

Orwell never intended *Nineteen Eighty-Four* to be his last book. But his health deteriorated so badly while he worked on it that he was destined not to complete another. During 1947 and 1948 he was often bedridden or hospitalized, and at last his condition was diagnosed as **tuberculosis**. By 1949, he was too ill to do much more than plan out a 'long short story' and write its first four pages. Then on 3 September, he was transferred from a **sanatorium** in Gloucestershire to University College Hospital, London.

His son, Richard, who had been with him and his sister Avril on Jura, could visit only rarely now – Orwell was terrified that the boy might catch his infection. 'He used to come to me and say, "Where have you hurt yourself?"' Orwell wrote to a friend. 'I suppose [it was] the only reason he could see for always being in bed.' But the patient did have other visitors – among them Sonia Brownell, an attractive, outspoken and intelligent woman whom Orwell had met several years before, possibly at the offices of the magazine *Horizon*. They had always been friendly, and in the summer of 1949 he proposed to her from his sickbed and she accepted.

Sonia Brownell (at front), who married Orwell just before he died, and later used his **pseudonym** as her own surname. Glamorous and lively, she was probably the inspiration for Winston Smith's lover, Julia, in *Nineteen Eighty-Four*. She died in 1980.

Both of them hoped this might give him a new lease of life, enabling him to survive for a few more years. They married in a short ceremony at Orwell's bedside in October 1949. But they were to be man and wife for just three months, and Orwell never came out of University College Hospital. On 21 January 1950 his lungs finally gave out and he died of **pulmonary** tuberculosis.

The man and his work

Towards the end of his life, Orwell made jottings in a notebook.
The last thing he wrote in it was: 'At 50, everyone has the face he
deserves.' He himself died at just 46 years of age. But in addition to
nine full-length books he left a rich legacy of essays, journalism and
letters. In 1968, the publishers Secker & Warburg published all this
material in four volumes, edited by Sonia Orwell (his second wife) and
Ian Angus. Interest in Orwell's fiction had continued, but these books
sparked a new and lasting appreciation of his non-fiction too.

'His was the guilty conscience of the educated and privileged man,'
wrote V. S. Pritchett in 1950, '...and this conscience could be **allayed**
only by taking upon itself the pain, the misery, the dinginess and the
pathetic but hard vulgarities of a stale and hopeless period'. Orwell
was a deeply serious man, with a deeply serious commitment to his
writing. Yet he brightened his often sombre work with flashes of dry
wit. Even when reviewing a translation of Hitler's grisly book *Mein
Kampf*, he remarked: 'The **Socialist** who finds his children playing
with soldiers is usually upset, but
he is never able to think of a
substitute for the soldiers; tin
pacifists somehow won't do.'

The crystal spirit

Like many driven men, Orwell
could be difficult to live with. He
made friends easily, but some of
those closest to him seemed to
respect rather than love him. He
could hardly blow his nose, said
Cyril Connolly, without moralizing
on conditions in the handkerchief
industry. And according to Lettice
Cooper, 'he was not in the least
interested in people except in
large political masses'.

George Orwell in 1945.

To his devoted later readers, George Orwell was little short of a saint – his every word striking a blow for decency, justice or common sense. Such a view might have startled Orwell. 'All writers are vain, selfish and lazy,' he declared, 'and at the very bottom of their motives there lies a mystery.' Yet he believed so passionately in the goodness of ordinary people, and he fought so hard for their cause, that this hardly seems to be true of him. In *Homage to Catalonia* he described shaking hands with an Italian

A well-stocked 'George Orwell' section in a 21st-century British bookshop.

militiaman. They met for only a moment and did not even speak the same language. But Orwell sensed a common humanity, a true bond of affection that countless readers have felt with Orwell himself. Later he wrote a verse to describe the emotion he felt in that moment:

'But the thing I saw in your face
No power can disinherit:
No bomb that ever burst
Shatters the crystal spirit.'

"
'Orwell could have made his life easier by writing in a prose style which was less demanding. But in all his work he drove himself relentlessly to resist the weaknesses which he describes in "Politics and the English Language" [see page 48]. Although writing did not have to be so exhausting, he chose to make it so because he found that he was bound to give as much of himself to his writing as he could. This was an old-fashioned notion, and perhaps a few years of psychiatric therapy could have cured him of it. Instead he created an enormous body of prose which, at its best, sings. And in large part he achieved this because – quite simply – he thought it was the right thing to do.'
From *Orwell – The Authorised Biography*, Michael Shelden (1991)

The influence of Orwell

In 1970, the publisher Fredric Warburg was asked his opinion of Orwell as a writer. He replied: 'I would say without hesitation that, with [D. H.] Lawrence, he was the best and most influential writer between 1930 and 1950, possibly 1960; that his work is gathering strength if you can judge by sales… He had a way of seeing through the appearance, of penetrating to the kernel of the argument, the nub of the thing, and putting it down.'

Orwell's influence is still felt in these two ways – in the clarity of his vision and in the clarity of his writing. 'Good prose,' he once wrote, 'is like a window pane'. He wanted his readers to be able to look through his own words to what he believed to be the essential truth.

The books in which Orwell's vision and prose were clearest were his last two, *Animal Farm* and *Nineteen Eighty-Four* – the first a political fable, the second a political **satire**. Both contained dark warnings about the abuse of power, and the latter gave a nightmarish glimpse of a society under ruthless **totalitarian** control. So powerful was this work that people still use the word 'Orwellian' to describe any aspect of modern life that reminds them of the bleak and menacing atmosphere conjured up in his later fiction. Inspired by Orwell, too, a number of novelists in Britain and abroad have written about their own 'dystopias' – imaginary worlds where everything is as bad as possible. Few of them, however, shared Orwell's profound political purpose in writing, and none could match the masterly way in which he used the English language.

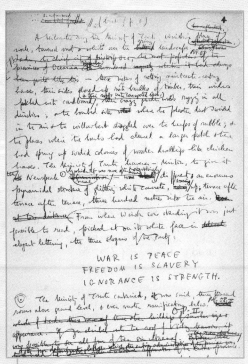

A handwritten page from an early draft of Orwell's masterpiece *Nineteen Eighty-Four*.

As an **epigraph** to his 1939 novel *Coming Up For Air*, Orwell used a line from a popular song: 'He's dead, but he won't lie down.' The same could be said of its author. Although Orwell died in 1950, his work is regularly quoted in debates about politics, literature and the nature of English society.

The passing traveller

V. S. Pritchett once said that Orwell 'belongs to no group, he joins no side... He is entirely on his own... rashly, almost bleakly, almost colourlessly and uncomfortably on his own.' To Orwell, that would have been a compliment. He always set a very high value on knowing his own mind. Sometimes that brought him into conflict with others. At others his writing could make people reassess or even change their own opinions.

When writing about *Animal Farm*, he wondered if his negative view of Stalin's **USSR** would one day become the **orthodox** one. (In fact it did, later in the **Cold War**.) 'But what use would that be in itself?' he asked. 'To exchange one orthodoxy for another is not necessarily an advance. The enemy is the gramophone mind, whether or not one agrees with the record that is being played at the moment.' Orwell unforgettably showed what can happen if people stop thinking for themselves or acting on their own beliefs. He warned that by becoming too passive, they could lose all chance of shaping the world they live in. That led V. S. Pritchett to write in his *New Statesman* obituary of Orwell: 'He has gone, but in one sense, he always made this impression of the passing traveller who meets one on the station, points out that one is waiting for the wrong train and vanishes.' Orwell's timeless reminder lives on in his work.

Timeline

1903	Born on 25 June as Eric Arthur Blair in Motihari, India.
1907	Mother brings him to England, where family settles in Thames Valley.
1911	Sent to St Cyprian's school in Eastbourne, Sussex.
1914–18	World War I.
1914	First work published: a poem in the *Henley and South Oxfordshire Standard*.
1916	Leaves St Cyprian's at Christmas.
1917	Enters Eton College as a **King's Scholar**. **Russian Revolution** begins.
1921	Leaves Eton College. Family moves to Southwold in Suffolk.
1922	Joins Indian Imperial Police in Burma, with intention to be a writer. In Italy **Fascists** under Benito Mussolini come to power.
1924	Joseph Stalin rises to undisputed mastery of the **Communist USSR**.
1927	Spends autumn of 1927 making first expeditions to investigate the plight of the poor in southern England.
1928	Leaves Indian Imperial Police on 1 January while on holiday with family in England.
1928–29	Lives in Paris, doing various jobs and attempting to write. First articles published in the press.
1930–32	Based in Southwold, continues investigations of how the poor live, while writing for journals, teaching and **hop**-picking to make money. Victor Gollancz accepts *Down and Out in Paris and London* for publication.
1933	*Down and Out in Paris and London* published in Britain and USA under **pseudonym** of George Orwell. While teaching in Uxbridge, Middlesex, completes *Burmese Days* and then almost dies of pneumonia. Adolf Hitler and Fascist Nazi Party come to power in Germany.

1934 Based again at the family home in Southwold, writes
A Clergyman's Daughter.
Burmese Days is published in USA.
Moves to London and takes job as part-time assistant in
Hampstead bookshop.

1935 *A Clergyman's Daughter* is published in Britain, then *Burmese
Days* is published in Britain (after Orwell's alterations, to
avoid the possibility of **libel**). Continues to write reviews
and articles.

1936 *A Clergyman's Daughter* is published in USA.
Completes *Keep the Aspidistra Flying*, which is published in
Britain in April.
Leaves Hampstead bookshop to research plight of the poor
and unemployed in northern England under **commission**
from Victor Gollancz.
Becomes grocer at The Stores in Wallington, Hertfordshire.
Marries Eileen O'Shaughnessy.
Submits *Shooting an Elephant* to *New Writing* magazine.
Spanish Civil War breaks out in July; in December, Orwell
enlists in POUM **militia** in Barcelona, Spain and fights on the
Aragon front.

1937 Is wounded in the throat in May and returns to Wallington.
In March *The Road to Wigan Pier*, an account of researches in
the north in 1936, is published in Britain.
Writes *Homage to Catalonia*, which Fredric Warburg contracts
to publish.

1938 Becomes seriously ill with tubercular lesion in one lung. On
medical advice, and with financial help from an **anonymous**
benefactor, he and Eileen spend time in the warmer climate
of Morocco.
Starts writing *Coming Up For Air*.
Homage to Catalonia is published in Britain.

1939 Completes *Coming Up For Air*, which is published in June
in Britain.
Returns to Wallington and writes essays and journalism while
working the plot of land alongside The Stores.
Outbreak of World War II in September. Despite repeated
efforts, he is unable to serve his country in any capacity due
to poor health.

1940 Relatively unproductive time; plans three-part family saga, which remains unwritten.
Inside the Whale published in Britain.
Moves to London, serving in the **Home Guard**.

1941 *The Lion and the Unicorn* published in Britain.

1941–43 Employed as Talks Producer for BBC Eastern Service.
Continues to write essays and journalism.

1943 Becomes literary editor of the *Tribune* in November 1943.
Begins to write *Animal Farm*.

1944 Completes *Animal Farm* but takes many months to find a publisher for it (eventually Fredric Warburg in Britain agrees to publish it).
Adopts son, Richard Horatio Blair.

1945 While he is in Europe reporting on the end of World War II, Eileen dies.
Employs Susan Watson to look after Richard.
Animal Farm is published in Britain in August.
Pays first visit to his retreat on the Scottish island of Jura.

1946 Despite poor health, spends several months on Jura with Richard, looked after by his sister Avril, working on the book that would become *Nineteen Eighty-Four*. *Animal Farm* is published with great success in USA.

1947–48 Divides time between Jura and London.
Chest specialist diagnoses **tuberculosis** of left lung.

1948 Orwell completes *Nineteen Eighty-Four*.
Enters **sanatorium** in Gloucestershire.

1949 As his health deteriorates, *Nineteen Eighty-Four* is published in Britain and USA simultaneously and is a huge success on both sides of the Atlantic.
Marries Sonia Brownell in September, while hospitalized in London.

1950 Dies on 21 January of **pulmonary** tuberculosis and is buried in churchyard of All Saints in Sutton Courtenay, Berkshire.

Glossary

administration day-to-day running of a country

advance sum of money paid 'up front' by a publisher to an author, so that he or she can write a book

aesthetic in accordance with principles of beauty and good taste

agent (literary) person who makes deals on behalf of authors with publishers, to get their books into print

allayed diminished, made more bearable

allegory description of one subject under the guise of another

anonymously without being named

anthology choice collection of writings

apocalyptic great and usually terrifying vision of the future

bird-nesting finding birds' nests and taking the eggs as trophies

Blitz (from German word *Blitzkrieg*, meaning 'lightning war') German air raids on London in 1940

British Empire enormous empire ruled over by Britain, which reached its greatest extent in the early 20th century, when around one fifth of the world's land mass, from Canada to South Africa and India to Australia, was under British rule

Cold War period extending for over four decades after World War II, when the Communist East (dominated by the USSR) confronted the democratic West (dominated by the USA), but did not get involved in actual 'hot' warfare

commission (verb and noun) agreement between an editor and an author that a piece of work should be written and paid for

Communist/Communism revolutionary Socialist creed which argues that each person should work for the common benefit according to his or her ability, and receive rewards according to his or her needs. The first Communist state, founded on the beliefs of the philosopher Karl Marx, was the USSR (1917–91). While admirable in its principles, Communism often proved to be brutally unfair in practice.

creed set of opinions or principles on any subject

dengue fever infectious tropical fever causing acute pain in joints

dictatorship rule by a 'dictator', who runs a country without taking any notice of the true wishes of its people, and usually prevents the people from making their wishes known at elections

dominion control, mastery

egoism self-centredness

epigraph inscription at start of book or chapter

eunuch man whose sexual organs have been removed

evacuated moved from dangerous place to a safer one

Fascist type of totalitarian system of beliefs in which individuals have no rights and the government has total power. In 1919 the Fascists under Benito Mussolini came to power in Italy, and in 1933 the Fascist Nazi Party under Adolf Hitler came to power in Germany. Fascists were fundamentally opposed to Communists.

Great Depression world crisis sparked off by a huge economic collapse in the USA – the Wall Street Crash of 1929. Without US financial support in the decade that followed, many European countries experienced serious economic problems, with the poorest classes of society suffering the most.

high-flown sophisticated

Home Guard (also known as 'Dad's Army') British citizen army recruited to defend country against possible invaders

hop plant used in the manufacture of beer

hysterectomy operation to have all or part of the womb removed

integrity deep honesty

intriguing plotting for one's own ends

King's Scholar one of 70 bright boys each year at Eton College whose parents had to pay only small fees, since they had passed a special examination

Left Book Club book club started by Victor Gollancz in 1936, offering one new book each month at a bargain price to readers 'who desire to play an intelligent part in the struggle *for* World Peace and a better social and economic order, and *against* Fascism'

left-wing likely to be socialist in one's ideas

libel/libellous published statement about a person that is false and damages his or her reputation

Marxist see Communist

militia body of soldiers, often made up of ordinary, untrained people

nationalization the taking over of big industries by a government in an attempt to run them for the benefit of the whole population

nostalgia looking back at the past with emotional, positive feelings

obituary notice of someone's death in a newspaper

orthodox standard, currently-accepted opinion on something

partisanship supporting a cause with great determination

plover type of bird, often found wading in water

potboiler something of no particular quality or value

prejudice having an uninformed opinion about a thing or person

probationary on probation, serving a kind of apprenticeship

proletariat lowest class in a community, usually wage-earners (in *Nineteen Eighty-Four* Orwell called this class 'the proles')

propaganda information in the media that supports or advertises a particular point of view or set of beliefs

pseudonym fictitious name used by a writer who wishes to keep his or her true identity secret

pulmonary affecting the lungs

puttees supportive strips of cloth wound around the calf

racist abusive about a person's race

republic country with an elected government and a president instead of a king or queen

revenue total income

right-wing 'conservative', likely to be opposed to Socialism, preferring to keep (conserve) many aspects of society rather than change them

Russian Revolution overthrow of the Russian monarchy in 1917 by Communist revolutionaries led by Lenin, Trotsky and later Stalin, resulting in the creation of the USSR

sahib Indian term of respect, used when addressing white men

sanatorium type of hospital for the chronically ill or for people recovering from illness

sardonically mockingly

satire humorous writing that exposes something silly or unfair

scholarship place at a fee-paying school (usually won by passing an exam), for which the student does not have to pay, or pay much

shilling small old English coin; there were 20 shillings in £1

Socialism/Socialist political and economic movement that aimed to introduce a 'classless' society, in which power and wealth would be shared out more equally. Lenin, the Russian Revolutionary leader, wrote that 'Under Socialism all will govern in turn and will soon become accustomed to no one governing.'

solidarity standing shoulder-to-shoulder with others

suffragette campaigner for the right of women to vote (called 'suffrage'), which was not completely achieved until 1928

supercilious seeming superior, 'snooty'

surrealist writing (and art) that aimed to express the subconscious mind – for example, through dreams

totalitarianism form of party government that allows no rival parties, and usually demands total obedience of the people

tuberculosis infectious bacterial disease, especially affecting the lungs

unorthodoxy opinion about something that opposes the standard, currently held view

USSR (Union of Soviet Socialist Republics, sometimes also known as the Soviet Union) name given to Russia and its empire after the Revolution of 1917. It broke up in 1991.

work-in-progress piece of writing or art that is still being worked on

Places of interest and further reading

The George Orwell Archive, University College, London, is the most important source of information on Orwell. Its collection of material includes a large body of Orwell's manuscripts, personal papers and letters as well as photos and videotapes of film and TV productions relating to the author and his work.

Further reading

BOOKS BY GEORGE ORWELL (with British first publication dates)

Down and Out in Paris and London (Gollancz, 1933)

Burmese Days (Gollancz, 1935)

A Clergyman's Daughter (Gollancz, 1935)

Keep the Aspidistra Flying (Gollancz, 1936)

The Road to Wigan Pier (Gollancz, 1937)

Homage to Catalonia (Secker and Warburg, 1938)

Coming Up For Air (Gollancz, 1939)

Inside the Whale (Gollancz,1940)

The Lion and the Unicorn (Secker and Warburg, 1941)

Animal Farm (Secker and Warburg, 1945)

Critical Essays (Secker and Warburg, 1946)

Nineteen Eighty-Four (Secker and Warburg, 1949)

The Collected Essays, Journalism and Letters of George Orwell (4 vols), edited by Sonia Orwell and Ian Angus (Secker and Warburg, 1968)

BOOKS ABOUT GEORGE ORWELL

The Crystal Spirit: A Study of George Orwell, George Woodcock (Schocken Books USA, 1984)

George Orwell: A Life, Bernard Crick (Secker and Warburg, 1980)

Orwell, Raymond Williams (Fontana Books, 1971)

Orwell, The Authorised Biography, Michael Shelden (Heinemann, 1991)

Orwell Remembered, edited by Audrey Coppard and Bernard Crick (BBC, 1984)

The Unknown Orwell, Peter Stansky and William Abrahams (Constable, 1972)

Index